For Kay Harrison

My World of Words in Spanish copyright © Frances Lincoln Limited 1996
Text copyright © Debbie MacKinnon 1996
Photographs copyright © Frances Lincoln Limited 1996
Postcard illustration copyright © Frané Lessac 1990

First published in Great Britain in 1996 by
Frances Lincoln Limited, 4 Torriano Mews
Torriano Avenue, London NW5 2RZ

British Library Cataloguing in Publication Data
available on request

ISBN 0-7112-0985-5

Printed in Hong Kong

1 3 5 7 9 8 6 4 2

My World of Words In Spanish

Debbie MacKinnon
Photographed by
Geoff Dann

Introduced by Opal Dunn

FRANCES LINCOLN

How to use this book

This exciting picture book helps children to begin classifying their world. From colours which are easy for the child to recognise and sort, it leads on to numbers, shapes and sizes, opposites and finally noises.

It is an ideal book to take your child further in Spanish if you've already been using *300 First Words in Spanish* with them. If you have, it may be a good idea to start using *My World of Words in Spanish* by finding some of the things they already know in Spanish like a banana, a digger, a T-shirt and move on from there to new things and ideas.

If *My World of Words in Spanish* is the first book you have used in Spanish, I suggest you start with the animal noises (pages 110 –117). Children find it fascinating that different languages make animals say different things – an English cock says "cock-a-doodle-doo" and a Spanish one *kikiriki*. Animal noises are a fun way to help them realise that there are two ways to talk about the same thing.

Before you teach your child the Spanish for anything in the book be sure that they understand the meaning in English. If you are not sure that your child understands the concept of round or what 12 really represents, collect some things that will help, and let them feel and arrange them in shapes. Trying to learn both a new concept and a new language at the same time is difficult. It's much simpler to learn the idea first and afterwards learn the Spanish for it.

My World of Words in Spanish takes you beyond just naming objects. The language which goes with many pictures tells you more about them –

J90,032   £5-99 $\frac{468}{2421}$

"a red tomato" (*un tomate rojo*) – "an empty basket" (*una cesta vacía*). Your child will pick up the Spanish more quickly if you introduce it in two steps in much the same way as you did when they learned their own language – name the object first *una cesta* and then expand it to include the adjective *una cesta vacía*.

Ask "*¿Qué es eso?*" (What's this?). They should be able to reply "*una cesta*", even if you have to help them a little. Confirm what they have said back to them, saying "*Sí, una cesta*" (Yes, a basket) and continue, "*una cesta vacía*", putting a little stress on *vacía* (an empty basket). Don't be tempted to make any comment about an adjective being sometimes in front and sometimes after the noun or about the difference between masculine and feminine. A child will hear the differences and will soon work out the rules. Children are used to doing this in their own language – nobody told them the rules of grammar when they were learning to speak.

As you both get to know the contents of the book, try to use some of the language at other times to name things you can both see around you. For example say "*¡Mira, un triángulo – un sandwich!*" or "*¡Mira – seis peces!*".

Progress depends a lot on success which in turn motivates; so don't forget to praise effort as well as correctness. Learning Spanish should be fun and sharing a book like *My World of Words in Spanish* is a good way for your young child to start.

Opal Dunn

Contents

Colores
Colours

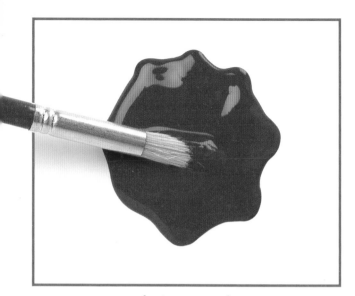

pintura roja
red paint

una fresa roja
red strawberry

un tomate rojo
red tomato

unas botas rojas
red boots

pintura azul
blue paint

un cubo azul
blue bucket

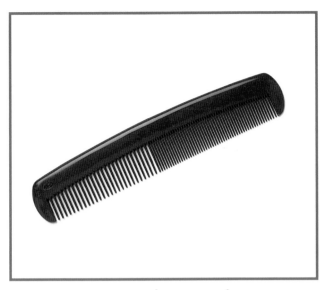

un peine azul
blue comb

unos pantalones vaqueros azules
blue jeans

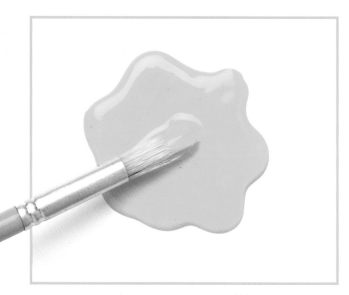

pintura amarilla
yellow paint

un pato amarillo
yellow duck

una flor amarilla
yellow flower

un plátano amarillo
yellow banana

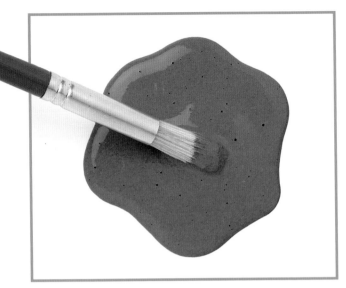

pintura verde

green paint

una rana verde

green frog

una manzana verde

green apple

una lechuga verde

green lettuce

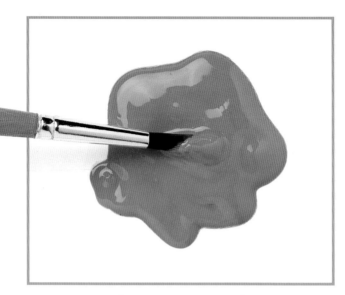

pintura naranja
orange paint

una naranja
orange

unas zanahorias de color naranja

orange carrots

unos calcetines de color naranja

orange socks

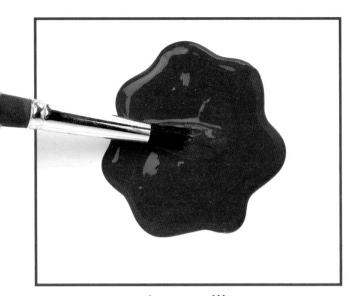

pintura lila
purple paint

un paraguas lila
purple umbrella

un lazo lila
purple bow

un chandal lila
purple sweatshirt

pintura negra
black paint

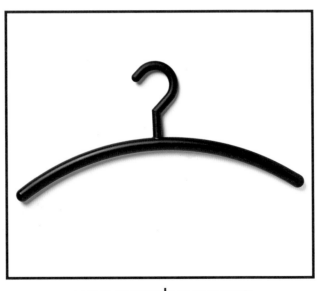

una percha negra
black hanger

una sartén negra

black frying pan

un gatito negro

black kitten

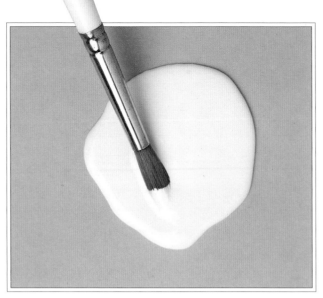

pintura blanca

white paint

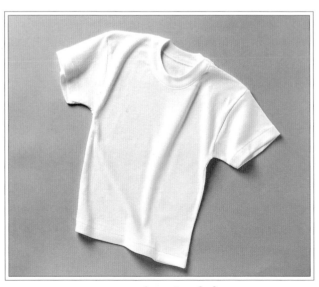

una camiseta blanca

white T-shirt

algodón blanco
white cotton wool

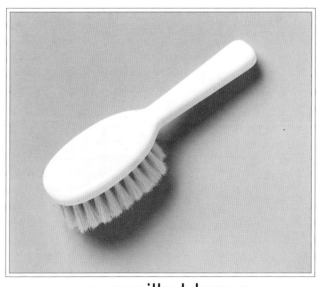

un cepillo blanco
white hairbrush

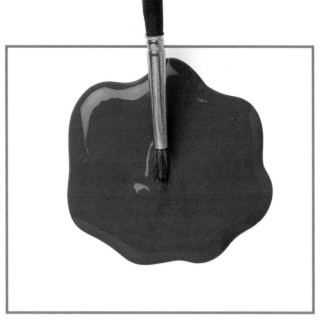

pintura marrón
brown paint

chocolate marrón
brown chocolate

un conejo marrón
brown rabbit

un bol marrón
brown bowl

pintura rosa
pink paint

unos leotardos de color rosa
pink tights

un esparadrapo rosa
pink plaster

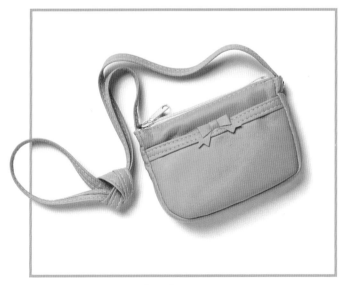

un bolso rosa
pink handbag

¡Mira cuantos rotuladores hay! ¿Cuántos colores puedes ver en el arco iris?

Look at all the coloured pens!
How many colours can you see
in the rainbow?

Números
Numbers

uno

one

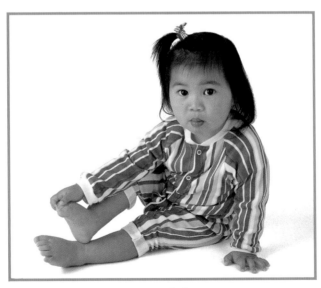

una chica

one girl

una taza
one cup

una silla
one chair

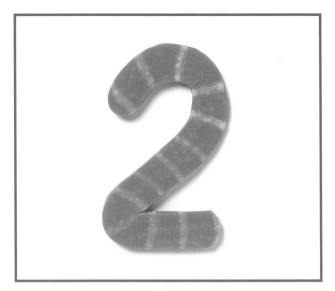

dos
two

dos gemelos
two twins

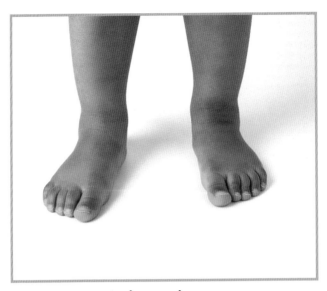

dos pies
two feet

dos zapatos
two shoes

tres

three

tres muñecas

three dolls

tres cerezas
three cherries

tres tenedores
three forks

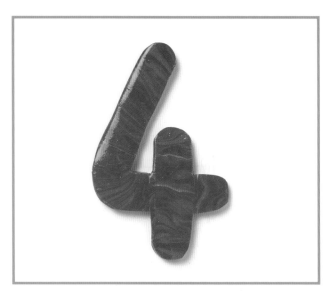

cuatro

four

cuatro canicas

four marbles

cuatro cepillos de diente
four toothbrushes

cuatro coches

four cars

cinco
five

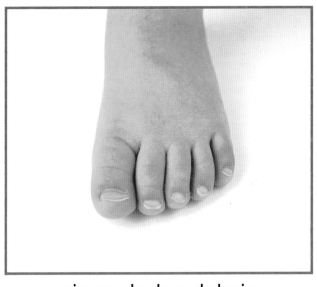

cinco dedos del pie
five toes

cinco hojas

five leaves

cinco guantes
five gloves

seis

six

seis pasas

six raisins

seis peces
six fish

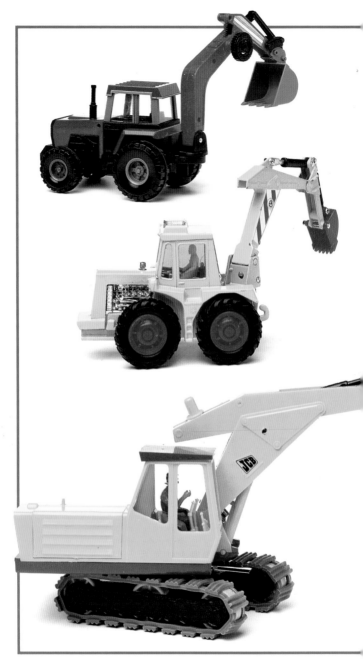

seis excavadoras
six diggers

siete
seven

siete mariquitas
seven ladybirds

siete barcos

seven boats

siete balones
seven balls

ocho
eight

ocho piedras
eight pebbles

ocho cucharas
eight spoons

ocho conchas
eight shells

nueve

nine

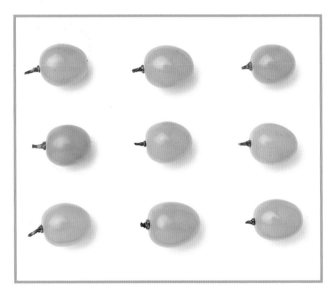

nueve uvas

nine grapes

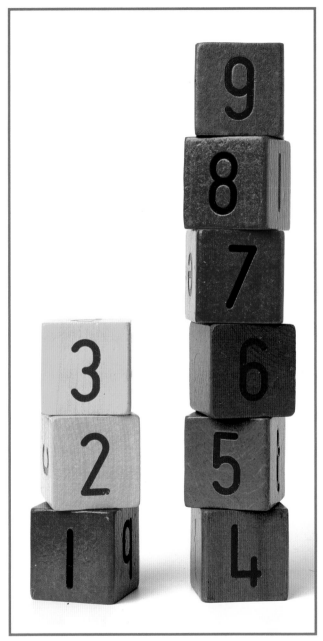

nueve bloques
nine bricks

nueve globos
nine balloons

diez
ten

diez dedos
ten fingers

diez lápices de cera
ten crayons

diez dinosaurios
ten dinosaurs

once

eleven

once botones

eleven buttons

doce

twelve

doce caramelos

twelve sweets

¡Mira cuantos juguetes hay!
¿Puedes contar los 3 balones,
las 2 excavadoras y la muñeca?

Look at all the toys!
Can you count 3 balls,
2 diggers and 1 doll?

Formas
Shapes

redondo
round

un plato
plate

un balón
ball

un pastel
cake

cuadrado
square

un bloque de tela
soft block

un rompecabezas
jigsaw puzzle

una fotografía
photograph

un triángulo

triangle

un sandwich

sandwich

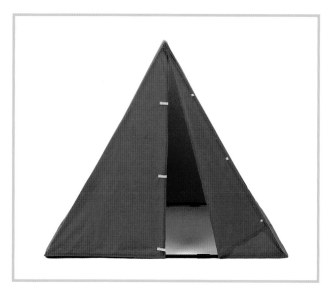

una tienda de campaña
tent

una porción de pizza
slice of pizza

un rectángulo
rectangle

un sobre
envelope

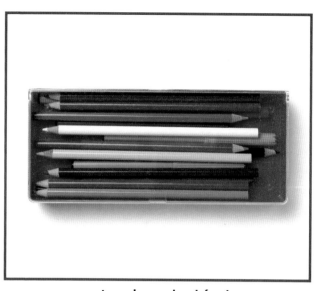

un estuche de lápices
pencil case

una postal
postcard

un oval
oval

un huevo
egg

una esponja

sponge

una piña

pine cone

un diamante
diamond

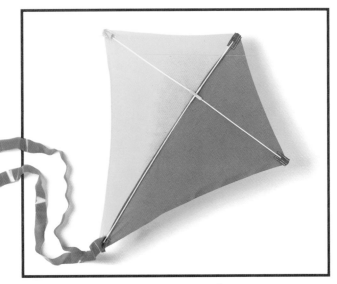

una cometa
kite

unos pendientes

earrings

unos chocolates

chocolates

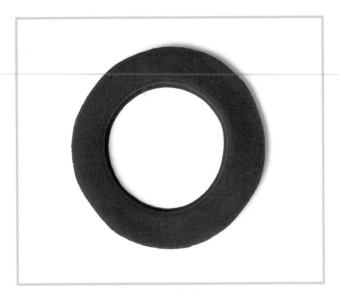

un anillo
ring

un donut
doughnut

un flotador
rubber ring

una pulsera
bracelet

un corazón
heart

una galleta
biscuit

un colgante
locket

jabón
soap

una estrella
star

una varita mágica
magic wand

una estrella de mar
starfish

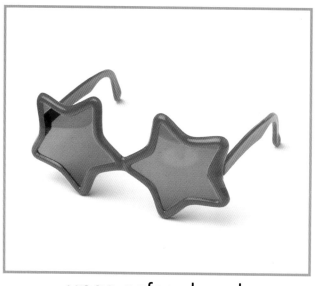

unas gafas de sol
sunglasses

un semicírculo
semicircle

un gorro
hat

una sandía
watermelon

un monedero
purse

¡Mira cuantas formas hay en
este payaso!
¿Qué formas puedes ver?
Look at all the shapes
in this clown!
What shapes can you see?

Opuestos
Opposites

un regalo grande
big present

un regalo pequeño
little present

un bebé grande
big baby

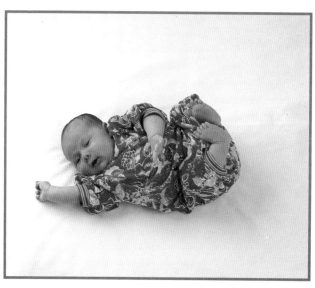

un bebé pequeño
little baby

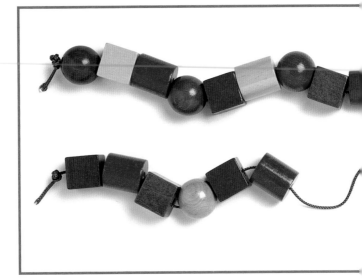

un collar corto de cuentas
short string of beads

un tren corto
short train

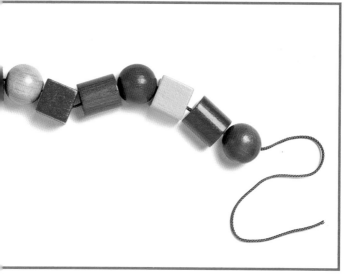

un collar largo de cuentas
long string of beads

un tren largo
long train

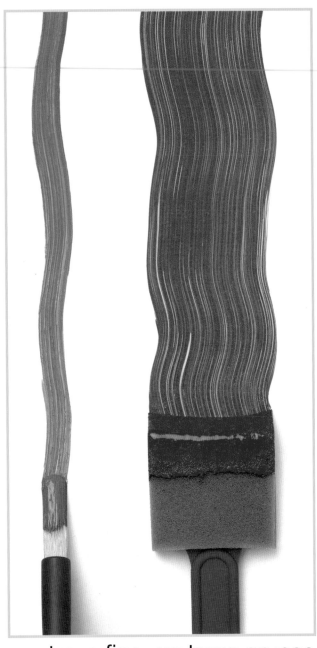

un trazo fino   un trazo grueso

thin line   thick line

un libro fino
thin book

un libro gordo
thick book

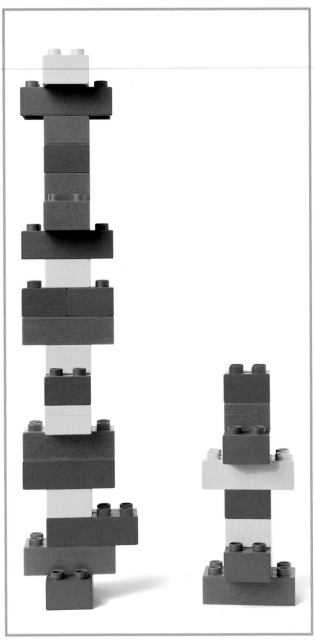

una torre alta
tall tower

una torre baja
small tower

un niño bajo
small boy

una niña alta
tall girl

limpio
clean

sucio
dirty

delante
front

detrás
back

una tacita llena
full beaker

una tacita vacía
empty beaker

una cesta llena
full basket

una cesta vacía
empty basket

vieja
old

joven
young

abierto
open

cerrado
closed

una silla alta

highchair

una silla baja
low chair

dormida

asleep

despierta

awake

contenta
happy

triste
sad

¡Mira cuantos ositos hay! ¿Cuál es el más grande? ¿Cuál es el más pequeño?

Look at all the teddy bears!
Which one is the biggest?
Which is the littlest?

Ruidos
Noises

guau guau
woof woof

miau
meow

brr
squawk

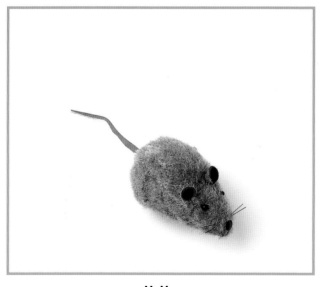

ii ii
squeak squeak

muu

moooo

oink oink

oink oink

bee bee
baa baa

iii
neigh

sss

hissss

brraa

terump-teraa

roarrr

roarrr

chi chi chi

chi chi chi

coc coc
cluck cluck

cua cua
quack quack

pio pio
cheep cheep

kikiriki!
cock-a-doodle-doo!

tatararí
toot toot

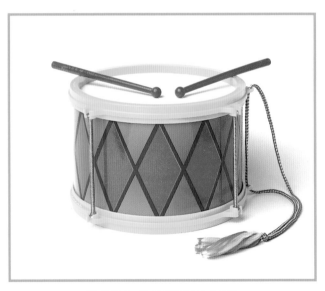

pom porropom
bang bang

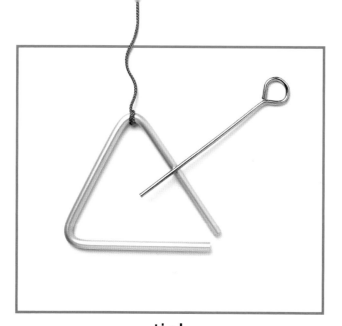

tin!
ting!

tin tin tin
ding-a-ling

tic tac

tick-tock

rin rin

brring-brring

rum rum
varooom

clic
click

¡Mira cuantas cosas ruidosas hay!
¿Cuál hace más ruido?

Look at all the noisy things!
Which one makes the
loudest noise?

Index